Winning at Work is filled with biblical principles that, if lived out, will help readers achieve greater success at work.

> —Chuck Buck,
> CEO, Buck Knives

Winning at Work is a powerful tool for all people wanting to find more purpose and fulfillment on their jobs.

> —Chuck Bengochea,
> CEO, Honey Baked Hams

You will never view your work in the same way after reading *Winning at Work.*

> —Matt McPherson,
> CEO, Matthews Bows

winning
AT
WORK

COURT
DURKALSKI

COURT DURKALSKI

winning
AT
WORK

Finding Greater Fulfillment
& Purpose On Your Job

Oviedo, Florida

Winning At Work: Finding Greater Fulfillment & Purpose On Your Job

by Court Durkalski
Published by HigherLife Development Services, Inc.
400 Fontana Circle
Building 1 – Suite 105
Oviedo, Florida 32765
(407) 563-4806
www.ahigherlife.com

Cover Design: r2cdesign—Rachel Lopez
First Edition
10 11 12 13 — 9 8 7 6 5 4 3 2 1
Printed in the United States of America

Dedicated to my wife, Amy—the love and joy of my life—and to my sons, Trevor and Aaron, who have made me proud to be their father.

ACKNOWLEDGMENTS

SPECIAL THANKS TO MY parents, Frank and Joan Durkalski, for teaching me personal responsibility and the merits of having a good work ethic. Thank you for instilling in me the values of respect and discipline. I also want to express appreciation to my wife's parents, Dan and Sally Needham, for entrusting me with their precious daughter, Amy, and for their encouragement through the years. I am grateful to my mentor, Carl Moellering, for showing me what it means to be a leader. In addition, I want to thank the Reverend Stefan Sawczak for teaching me what it means to be a follower of Jesus. I would like to thank Jeff Abbe and Tom Owens (and countless others) who prayed for me. I would also like to thank the employees and leadership team at Truline Industries, Inc.—Stuart, Tom, Don, Mike, Alan, Betsy, and others—for their willingness to believe in me. And, lastly, this book may have never been written had it not been for the encouragement of Hal Donaldson.

FOREWORD

I N THE TWENTY-FIRST CENTURY, it is not uncommon to find Christians who struggle to manage their businesses and do their work in a godly way. Sometimes we as Christians may even wonder if it is possible. I want to tell you that it is. I believe that God's plan for us is to be the salt and light not only in our daily lives, but also in the business community in which we work. In order to fulfill this plan, we must deliberately choose to run our businesses and serve in the workplace based on biblical truths. While we are in this world, we are not of this world. Once we understand this concept, we can begin to put into the workplace the effective principles found in God's Word. *Winning at Work* is a book that gives you a practical, easy-to-follow guide that will help you understand the benefits of ensuring that your work and business are built on a biblical foundation.

—Anne Beiler

Founder, Auntie Anne's Pretzels

CONTENTS

"One of the things that we have failed to understand is that God made us holistic. He never allows us to segment our lives like we do. We say, 'Well, this is my work, this is my church, this is my home, this is my personal life.' Whatever we are, we are wherever we are."

—Henry Blackaby

INTRODUCTION

I F A HALL OF Fame were created for the planet's most prolific workers, my father would be inducted on the first ballot. Even though the placard on his door read "President/CEO" of Truline Industries, Inc., and he had earned the right to spend his afternoons on the golf course, he chose to lead his employees by example. He often worked twelve-hour days, seven days a week, to build a successful jet parts manufacturing business that would provide well-paying jobs for his employees and a comfortable lifestyle for his family. Whatever the task, he gave 100 percent. He could operate every piece of equipment on the factory floor and occasionally joined the employees on the assembly line. For him, hard work was a privilege—not an obligation.

Unfortunately I didn't inherit his work ethic. For years, I viewed work as the enemy—something to be avoided. If someone had requested my definition of "pain," I would have described it as spending 50 or

60 hours a week in an office pushing a pencil, with a phone connected to my ear and a computer screen and keyboard staring me in the face. Work was right up there with root canals and bouts of the flu.

Because my father was my employer, I was often AWOL when the work bell rang. And, during work hours, my eyes were fixed on the clock like a weary boxer pleading for the final round to end. I couldn't wait to unlace my work gloves and step outside the ring. Years ago, no one could have imagined I would author a book on the virtues of work. That would be akin to Donald Trump writing a book entitled *The Art of Mediocrity in the Workplace.*

But when I began to study the teachings of Jesus, changes began to take place in my life, including my work habits. I discovered what my father already knew: work is not a curse on humanity. In fact, it is a gift from the Creator. He intended for us to enjoy work, to find fulfillment and purpose through our labors. As it says in Psalm 90:17, "May the favor of the Lord our God rest upon us; establish the work of our hands for us—yes, establish the work of our hands."

Work, however, causes many people tremendous anxiety and turmoil. Work-related issues have been known to cause health problems, family breakups, emotional disorders and more. If not approached properly, work-related issues can paralyze us and lead to unnecessary stress and depression.

Studies indicate that job satisfaction has declined across all income brackets for nine consecutive years.[1] Night after night, after a long day at work, many people collapse onto the couch in their living rooms and say, "I hate my job—just once I'd like to tell my boss to take this job and shove it. I give 100 percent and get no appreciation." But, the foundational message of this book is that work can be an enriching and joyful experience.

Often at the root of discouragement and frustration on the job is a poor understanding of the important part the Creator intended work to play in our lives. And, in difficult economic times, when competition for jobs is highest and unemployment rates are climbing, workers need to have proper perspective. Their success and longevity in the workplace depend on it.

Winning at Work contains job-related principles that will shape one's outlook on work, foster a new appreciation for employers and coworkers, and help employees find greater satisfaction in their daily tasks. Moreover, this book is a reminder that our labor is a form of worship to the Creator. Like a film director watching his actors, or an athletic coach observing his players, God delights in our performance on the job. In turn, He promises to reward us with something far more valuable than a pay raise or hall of fame nomination. He promises His favor and undeniable presence.

CHAPTER 1

GETTING MOTIVATED TO WORK

As a youth, Friday was my favorite day of the week. It was the day I collected my paycheck and the day my weekend of partying began. Hearing the five o'clock bell and walking out the door was akin to a prisoner being released from his cell. I worked five days to earn enough money to do anything I wanted on the weekends, which often included abusing drugs and alcohol. My motivation for working was simple: I worked so I could play. I told myself, "I worked for it—so I can spend my money anyway I want to."

Today some employees view their job as a 40-hour prison sentence or obligation that robs them of fun and relaxation. After four hours of sleep and three cups of coffee, they drag themselves to work at 8 a.m. so they can pay their mortgage, take in a dinner and a movie each week, and afford a new car. They find virtually no fulfillment in their work and blame their dissatisfaction on their employer, job function, pay scale, work environment, coworkers, and more. But at the heart of their misery is a lack of understanding of a biblical definition of work.

Merriam-Webster's Collegiate Dictionary, eleventh Edition, defines work as "the labor, task or duty that is one's accustomed means of livelihood."[1] The Bible, on the other hand, provides a broader definition of work, fulfillment, and success. First Corinthians 10:31 says, "Whatever you do, do it all for the glory of God." In other words, our primary purpose in working is to bring glory to the Creator. That is all the motivation we should need. We find fulfillment and success on the job by worshiping Him through our work. Whether we are negotiating multimillion-dollar real estate deals or driving a garbage collection truck, we are to worship God through our labor.

Paying Bills

First Timothy 5:8 says providing financially for our family is a God-given responsibility: "If anyone does not provide for his relatives, and especially for his immediate family, he has denied the faith and is worse than an unbeliever." But we have been conditioned to believe the *only* reason we work is to provide for our families. God, however, has instructed us to work for reasons far beyond paying bills, having fun, or pleasing others. Here are five additional motivations to consider:

First, we work to be obedient to God. He wants us to understand that He alone is our Provider. Our employer is merely a human mechanism that He uses to deliver our wages. **(See Psalm 111:5.)**

Second, we work so God can develop character and discipline in us and expand our capacity for the challenging tasks to come. **(See Colossians 3:23, 24.)**

Third, we work so we can contribute financially to God's work and help those who are less fortunate. **(See Luke 14:13, 14.)**

Fourth, we work because God has projects He wants to accomplish through our labors. He certainly does not need our help, but He gives us the privilege of partnering with Him to meet needs. **(See 1 Corinthians 3:6-9.)**

Fifth, we work because it strengthens our relationships with coworkers and gives us an opportunity to exemplify Christ in the marketplace. **(See Matthew 5:16.)**

God leads us by example. He has not commanded us to work while He remains inactive. He is not a Creator who merely observes our labors from His throne and coaches from the sidelines. He is a motivated God—constantly at work in the world and in our lives. Psalm 19:1 says, "The heavens declare the glory of God; the skies proclaim the work of his hands."

Garden of Eden

When God created the Garden of Eden, He assigned tasks to Adam. Genesis 2:15 says, "The Lord God took the man and put him in the Garden of Eden to work it and take care of it." The Hebrew translation of "work" uses the words *abad* (to serve, work or worship) and *shamar* (to keep watch or guard). Some theologians have interpreted this scripture to mean that we worship God by working or tending to His creation.

Our paradigm needs to shift from work to worship. Worship has been relegated to 30 minutes of music on a Sunday morning, when God intended for it to be every moment of our lives. In the boardroom on Monday, a construction site on Tuesday, or in a classroom on Wednesday, our labor is worship to the Creator of the universe.

Work is not a by-product of sin, although following Adam's disobedience in Genesis 3:17-19, our labor certainly became more difficult: "To Adam he said, 'Because you listened to your wife and ate from the tree about which I commanded you, "You must not eat of it." Cursed is the ground because of you; through painful toil you will eat of it all the days of your life. It will produce thorns and thistles for you, and you will eat the plants of the field. By the sweat of your brow you will eat your food until you return to the ground.'"

Work became more burdensome because, through his disobedience, Adam separated himself from God. The Creator intended work to be relational—a cooperative effort between Him and His creation. He intended work to be more about strengthening that bond and less about the results or outcome of our labor. We can enjoy a semblance of what Adam had with God in the garden if we are willing to submit our will to God, view our circumstances from His perspective, and see our work as a form of worship.

Years ago, I manned a piece of equipment on our factory floor. Eight hours a day I worked alone producing jet parts. It didn't take me long, however, to discover I needed interaction with something other than a machine. At the end of the day, I needed more than the fulfillment of producing my daily quota of jet parts. I much preferred being assigned to work alongside another employee—someone with whom I could interact. From my vantage point, the parts I manufactured were temporary, but the relationship built with a coworker was eternal. In similar fashion, God wants us to value work as a way of nurturing our relationship with Him.

We were created to work *and* worship. Unfortunately we tend to focus more on the work than on the worship. But our work becomes a privilege and a beautiful form of worship when our focus and purpose in life are aligned with the Creator. When we are aligned with Him, we can experience fulfillment and success wherever we are called to serve: The attorney can sense God's presence in the midst of a hotly contested case; the school teacher can find comfort when students are unmanageable; the contractor can find wisdom when negotiating with an unreasonable customer; the housewife can find fulfillment when staring at a house full of chores.

Ecclesiastes 2:24 is a reminder that when we find pleasure in our work, we please God and fulfill His purposes: "A man can do nothing better than to eat and drink and find satisfaction in his work. This too, I see, is from the hand of God."

Challenges in the workplace make us navigate through each day with a smile etched on our face. But the smile on God's face never fades when, in good days and bad, we worship Him through our work.

ASK YOURSELF

What steps can I take to start my job each morning with more enthusiasm?

ACTION PLANS

1. Write a personal letter of gratitude to God for providing you with a job.

2. Ensure that you are designating at least 10 percent of your earnings to God's work.

APPLICATION PRAYER

Dear God: Thank You for giving me a job and the abilities to do that job. I confess that I have not always been grateful for my employment. May I see work as a privilege instead of an obligation. I want my work to bring glory and honor to You. I commit my job and my future to You. Amen.

"Our rich texture of racial, religious and political diversity will be a Godsend in the 21st century. Great rewards will come to those who can live together, learn together, work together, forge new ties that bind together."

— *President Bill Clinton*

CHAPTER 2

WORKING FOR THE RIGHT BOSS

HALF OF THE WORKERS in the United States, according to a survey, do not respect their supervisor and classified their boss as "incompetent." Less than 30 percent believe their bosses are fulfilling their responsibilities as motivators, role models, and mentors.[1] In Britain, 77 percent of the respondents to a survey indicated they believe their boss is not truly interested in their well-being.[2]

Considering these statistics, is it any surprise there is a crisis in work relations? Mounting distrust between management and the workforce, along with economic uncertainties, have given rise to picket lines, lockouts, and the shipment of jobs overseas. In some cases, these conflicts could have been avoided if workers held more respect for their boss's authority and employers showed more concern for their workers' well-being.

At one time I too did not respect my boss's authority. My father was the President/CEO of the company, and yet I challenged him at every turn. After all, we were trying to operate a company on Christian principles and I was the one with the Bible college degree. At times, I thought I knew more than he did and didn't hesitate to let him know. But one day all that changed.

I attended a conference for business leaders when the speaker posed a question to the audience: "How many of you are submitted to God?" Virtually every person in the room, including me, raised his or her hand. "Now," he asked, "how many of you are submitted to your CEO?" I couldn't raise my hand. He said, "If you are not submitted to your CEO, you're not fully submitted to God."

The speaker proceeded to read Romans 13:1-5: "Everyone must submit himself to the governing authorities, for there is no authority except that which God has established. The authorities that exist have been established by God. Consequently, he who rebels against the authority is rebelling against what God has instituted, and those who do so will bring judgment on themselves."

That afternoon the conference speaker reminded us that the Apostle Paul was writing in reference to a

Roman government that stood in violent opposition to Christianity and Judaism. This government was a far cry from democratic rule, and held little regard for the rights of non-Romans. Thus, in this passage, Paul instructs us to submit to *all* authority—not just godly leadership. For followers of Jesus, submission to a boss is not optional.

The Apology

When I returned from the conference I walked into my father's office. "Dad," I said with tears surfacing, "I love you and I want to ask for your forgiveness. I have not been fully submitted to you and your authority. I've been wrong. But from this day forward, I promise that I'm going to serve you and do whatever I can to accomplish the objectives you believe God has for this company; and it no longer matters whether I ever serve as CEO of Truline. My focus is to serve you and serve the Lord."

With tears streaming down his cheeks, he said, "I love you, son. I'm proud of you." He stepped out from behind his desk and we embraced as fathers and sons should. That day marked a change in our working relationship. Never again did I challenge his authority. And, in a sense, it was a day of liberation—

because I knew I was honoring God by showing respect to my CEO. Within a year of that spiritual breakthrough, my father announced his retirement and named me CEO.

Many assume they work for the person signing their paycheck—a president, a treasurer, a supervisor, a business owner. In reality, we work for God and freely offer our time and talent to our employer. In other words, God is the "right" boss.

Submission to an employer, however, does not suggest that we should allow ourselves to become a doormat to an inconsiderate, demeaning boss. Rather, reasonable submission is an act of love, an understanding that all authority comes from God. And He has placed us under an employer for a reason— though it may not be easy and be only for a season. We can rest in the knowledge that—regardless of the size of our paycheck or job title—we are serving an employer whom God has called us to honor.

Colossians 3:22-25 calls us to submission: "Slaves, obey your earthly masters in everything; and do it, not only when their eye is on you and to win their favor, but with sincerity of heart and reverence for the Lord. Whatever you do, work at it with all your heart, as working for the Lord, not for men, since you know that you will receive an inheritance from the Lord as a reward."

Radical Servanthood

In the Bible, David understood the concept of radical servanthood. He was anointed king as a young man and yet, for many years, he served faithfully under an ungodly leader—King Saul. Despite Saul's personal attacks and threats, David did not retaliate by attempting to maneuver politically or force himself onto the throne. Instead, he waited on God for his promotion and thus experienced Divine favor.

What can we learn about submission from David's example when we find ourselves in opposition to the decisions, policies, or actions of our employer? Here are five modern day responses:

1. Saying "Yes, sir" or "Yes, ma'am" when everything within you begs to declare your opposition.

2. Agreeing to work overtime to help a supervisor accomplish a task you think is unnecessary or may bring you no credit.

3. Allowing a supervisor to take credit for your idea.

4. Choosing not to retaliate when mistreated, overlooked, or under appreciated by a supervisor. (See Romans 12:19, Hebrews 10:30.)

5. Defending your employer when he is unfairly criticized.

Submission is an act of humility. Christ modeled this humility when He permitted His captors to nail Him to the Cross. He could have summoned 10,000 angels to His rescue. Instead, He said, "Father, forgive them, for they do not know what they are doing" (Luke 23:34). He endured the Cross in obedience to the Father, so our sins could be forgiven and we could inherit the promise of eternal life. He endured the Cross because He loved us and wanted us to enjoy the splendor of heaven.

In obedience to our Master, we are called to persevere (or endure) in submission to those who have been placed in authority over us in the workplace.

In her book, *Brokenness*, Nancy Leigh DeMoss tells of her relationship with a Romanian pastor named Joseph Tson. During a ten-year exile from

Romania due to intense persecution, he studied the American church and found a few semantical problems with our beliefs. The first is the unwillingness to use the word *surrender* and the desire to use the word *commitment* instead. *Commitment* insinuates that I am in control, as opposed to *surrender*, which alludes to someone else being in control. Because of our fiercely independent spirit in America, we really struggle with the concept of surrendering to God. Tson takes it one step further with our substitution of the word *servant* for *slave*. Because of our rightly justified hatred of the concept of one human being owning another, we have altered the biblical concept of being a slave to God. The Greek word for slave is *doulos* and the Greek word for servant is *diakonos*. Our relationship to God is always referred to as *douleo* to God (slave to God) never as *diakoneo* to God (servant to God). The design God had in mind is for us to be in a slave relationship to God, completely surrendered to His will.... Slavery to God is freedom. What would it look like to be able to go to work and not worry about pay, advancement, benefits, competition, workload, relationships? I believe it would look like this: starting the day surrendered to God and trusting Matthew 6:33 and Eph. 6:7, "But seek first His kingdom and His righteousness, and all these things will be added to you," and "With good will render service, as to the Lord, and not to men." This aligns us with why we work and who and what we are to truly work for. If we have also surrendered where we are to work to His will, it allows us the peace to accept anything that comes our way during the work day because we know He has allowed it and it can be used for His glory.[3]

ASK YOURSELF

What can I do to express appreciation to my supervisor and/or employer?

ACTION PLANS

1. Pray each day for your supervisor and the president or owner of your company.

2. Regularly thank your supervisor for his or her leadership.

APPLICATION PRAYER

Dear God: Thank You for placing me in the service of my supervisor and the leaders of my company. Please give me a burden to pray for them. Help me die to my selfish nature and to be in proper submission to those in authority over me. Lord, I am working for You. May my diligence and excellence at work bring glory to Your name. Amen.

"The best way to appreciate your job is to imagine yourself without one."

—*Oscar Wilde*

Chapter 3

Coping with a Miserable Job

T HE TOP 10 REASONS employees gave for quitting their job were as follows:[1]

1. Management demanded personnel to do the work of two people.

2. Management ordered a reduction in administrative help.

3. Management froze salaries.

4. Management refused to empower workers.

5. Management displayed an inability to make decisions.

6. Management decided to relocate offices.

7. Management changed the company's direction.

8. Management communicated poorly to its employees.

9. Management promoted unqualified people.

10. Management fostered competition among departments.

It is noteworthy that the top 10 reasons in this survey pertained to management failures and none related to employee performance or attitude.

Another survey identified the four issues employees are least satisfied with at their company: the bonus plan, promotion policies, health coverage, and pension plan.

Certainly there is widespread dissatisfaction among workers. While it is easier to blame our misery on a supervisor, paycheck, coworker, or work environment, often our dissatisfaction is not related to work. It stems from a lack of understanding of God's purpose for our lives. Again, our natural focus tends to be on work rather than worship.

Society has not conditioned us to worship God; it has influenced us to worship ourselves. As a result, we tend to place a high value on our possessions, job status, comfort, security, and more. Meanwhile, servanthood, character, perseverance, sacrifice, and more fall toward the bottom of our priority list.

Two Questions

If we are miserable with our jobs, we need to ask ourselves two questions:

1. Are we working for God or working for ourselves?

2. Are we working where God has called us to serve?

When we are not working for God or not working where He has called us, the symptoms will be obvious: irritability, complaining, selfishness, defensiveness, retaliation, criticizing, playing the victim, and more.

Some Christians are miserable because they are trying to live up to others' expectations rather than to biblical standards. Some are dissatisfied because they can feel envy's tightening noose around their

necks, comparing their job, salary, and lifestyle
to others'. Their priorities have shifted. They now
yearn for more recognition and reward from their
employer. Advancement has become the goal rather
than growing in their relationship with Jesus and
trusting Him to guide their steps. Ultimately they
discover that the path they have chosen only leads to
more misery.

Years ago, a friend of mine was in a constant
state of dissatisfaction with his job. By all accounts,
his manager was trying to force him to quit by
making his work environment increasingly difficult.
Eventually my friend was demoted and some of his
privileges taken away. But rather than give his supervisor the satisfaction of accepting his resignation, he
remained on the job and resorted to complaining and
criticizing. Consequently his problems at work also
had a negative impact on his life at home and church.

Finally I asked, "Why don't you just quit?" He
replied, "Because I believe God wants me to be
there." Here was the problem with his perspective: If
he truly believed God had placed him in a job that
made him miserable, he had no right to complain
about his supervisor. If anywhere, his anger should
have been directed at God—his job placement
officer. Rather than curse his employer in private or

wave his fist behind his back, He should have raised his head toward heaven and said, "God, why have you forsaken me?"

And, if indeed he was that miserable with his job, we can assume he was not giving 100 percent to God and the employer. Unhappy employees seldom perform at their highest level.

When my friend became ill and couldn't work, the company threatened to lay him off. He was pondering a lawsuit against his employer when I advised him to ask God to help change his perspective. To his credit, he listened to my counsel, and kept his job. And, in the end, he learned we are never victims if we are working where God wants us. He discovered the meaning of 1 Thessalonians 5:18: "Give thanks in all circumstances, for this is God's will for you in Christ Jesus." And he learned that it is impossible to be miserable and express our gratitude to God at the same time.

Call to Contentment

As a young man who was not serving God, I was never content. I had to own the latest gadgets and newest models. I once owned a Porche 911 Coupe, worth $75,000. But one day a new 911 Cabriolet convertible pulled up next to my car. Instantly, owning a convertible became an obsession. Within a matter of days, I traded in the Coupe I had owned for three months for a new Cabriolet—just so I could experience the thrill of driving with the top down. Then, after a few months, discontent set in and I began looking for my next car. What I already owned was never enough. My insatiable appetite for something new led me to make poor decisions. Happiness and fulfillment were fleeting.

My life was a portrait of discontentment—a far cry from what the Apostle Paul wrote about in Philippians 4:11,12: "I have learned to be content whatever the circumstances I know what it is to be in need, and I know what it is to have plenty. I have learned the secret of being content in any and every situation, whether well fed or hungry, whether living in plenty or in want."

Frequently I hear from people who are not content with their current employment. Because they believe the grass is greener elsewhere, they inquire about job openings at Truline Industries. In most cases, they want me to help them change their circumstances— escape a difficult boss, get a deserved promotion, and more. Sometimes, in a gentle way, I suggest that they consider simply changing how they view their circumstances. Too often workers run from their jobs and fall out of God's perfect will. Without knowing it, by changing jobs, they are taking a detour from the path God chose for them.

Jonah is a biblical example of one who refused to follow God's leading and, as a result, he suffered the consequences. God instructed him to proceed to Ninevah and call the people to repentance. But Jonah had his own ideas, which eventually landed him in the belly of whale fighting for his life. Only when he stopped complaining and began worshiping God amid dire circumstances was He rescued. Ultimately, Jonah acknowledged he had made a mistake, he sought God's forgiveness, and he pledged to go wherever God took him. (See Jonah 2:1-9.)

God wants us to be content with whatever role He calls us to play in His kingdom—regardless of how large or small the role may appear in the eyes of others. God doesn't call His children to meaningless or insignificant jobs. In Romans 12:4-5, the Apostle Paul says, "Just as each of us has one body with many members, and these members do not all have the same function, so in Christ we who are many form one body, and each member belongs to all the others."

Pushing a Broom

Sometimes people see themselves as a CEO of a Fortune 500 company, when God has called them to serve Him by pushing a broom, working on an assembly line, or teaching in a classroom. Because they are dissatisfied with the role God has for them to play, they chastise their employer for not promoting them to a higher position. Discontentment is like poison in the workplace. Most companies deal swiftly with employees who are infecting other workers with restlessness and an attitude of entitlement. They understand that people who are hurting tend to hurt others.

If we allow unhappiness to rule in our hearts in the workplace, we walk out from under God's covering and blessing. Our lives should be a portrait of contentment—and our positive attitude exemplary—because we know we are where God has placed us.

If you are miserable on your job, memorize Romans 8:28: "And we know that in all things God works for the good of those who love him, who have been called according to his purpose." Remind yourself that God is at work on your behalf even when your work circumstances are threatening to steal your joy. You are not alone on the job. God is with you. Every day—regardless of what you face at work—you can walk onto your job with a smile and say, "God, let's do this together." It is more difficult to be miserable when we know God is by our side, listening to our words and monitoring our attitude.

ASK YOURSELF

Am I talking to more people than I should about my job dissatisfaction?

ACTION PLANS

1. Ask God to forgive us for our complaining and criticism.

2. Make a list of the things that make your job unfulfilling and difficult. Pray for God to adjust your attitude. Mark them off the list as God begins to deal with each issue on your behalf.

APPLICATION PRAYER

Dear God: Please forgive my complaining and improper attitude. Let my coworkers see a change in me. May I be used by You to influence them. Thank You for being by my side and working on my behalf. Amen.

"Choose a job you love, and you will never work a day in your life."

—*Chinese Proverb*

CHAPTER 4

FINDING THE
PERFECT JOB

For years my life was racing recklessly in the wrong direction. I didn't know—and didn't care—that God had a plan for my life. Upon graduating from high school, I moved into my own apartment and started hanging out with a group of people who consumed large quantities of alcohol and experimented with drugs. I started working for my father at Truline Industries and was paid more money than most kids my age. I used the money to buy alcohol and cars, including a supercharged Corvette I raced at a local drag strip.

After my parents bought me a "funny car," I began racing on the National Hot Rod Association circuit. As with most professional sports, there were lots of temptations. I was truly living in the fast lane—using drugs and running with fast women. I thought I had the perfect job. In reality the job and destructive lifestyle had me. For four years, I flew around the country to compete in drag races. In each city, I stayed in expensive hotels and hopped from one nightclub to another in Lamborghinis and Ferraris. When I look back now, it is ridiculous how much money I wasted. My cocaine habit alone was costing $1,000 per week.

Finally, my self-indulgent lifestyle, alcoholism, and deception caught up with me. And yet, despite a painful divorce, I continued lusting after all the world had to offer.

In 1987 I paid a visit to a travel agent, intending to book a vacation to somewhere the parties lasted through the night. Instead, the attractive travel agent invited me to accompany her on a cruise to the Caribbean. I was afraid of getting caught with cocaine in another country, so I convinced myself to leave the illegal substance behind. While on the cruise and temporarily off drugs, I began to see my life with greater clarity. I knew I needed to do everything possible to reconcile with the woman who had been my fiancée.

Upon returning from the cruise, it occurred to me that God might be able to help me get my fiancée back. In an attempt to earn His help, I went to a bookstore and bought three versions of the Bible and began reading them in parallel fashion. By the time I had read from Genesis to the Book of John, I knew I was lost and needed salvation. Alone in my living room, I confessed my sin, surrendered my life to Jesus, and made Him my Lord and Savior. That day I was also instantly delivered from cocaine and alcohol. I was never reunited with my fiancée, but gaining a relationship with Christ proved to be far more valuable.

The years of never being satisfied and always seeking more pleasure came to an abrupt end. The void in my life was replaced by a deep love for God. The distractions—such as Porsches and parties—also faded in importance. I just knew I needed more of Jesus.

A few days later, I heard that a former defensive end for the Detroit Lions and Cleveland Browns, Bill Glass, was speaking at an inspirational rally. I attended the first night, and then invited my father to come the second night. At the close of the church service, he rededicated his life to Christ. My mother, who seldom left the house due to some health issues, agreed to join us for the final night of the meetings. It was one of the greatest miracles I have ever witnessed when, in front of 5,000 people, she stood to her feet and committed her life to Jesus.

My life was completely transformed. I began to understand that I belonged to God and He created me for a purpose. My life was no longer my own. That was the beginning of my quest to discover God's plan for my life. As I matured in my faith and studied the Bible, I learned that obedience to God's call is a life-long journey. That journey does not end when we land on a particular vocation or place of employment. Each day requires that we ask Him to use our lives to accomplish His will. I discovered that finding "the perfect job" is less important than having an obedient heart.

Just as God called Barnabas and Saul, He calls you and me today to accomplish His work: "While they were worshiping the Lord and fasting, the Holy Spirit said, 'Set apart for me Barnabas and Saul for the work to which I have called them'" (Acts 13:2).

Our responsibility is to prepare ourselves—to sharpen our skills—and to be willing to accept whatever task God sets before us. Just as He prepared Nehemiah to build a wall and Noah to build an ark, He has a purpose for our lives. But we will never know our particular calling unless, like Nehemiah and Noah, we are in close relationship with God and recognize His voice when He speaks to our hearts.

Chasing Money

Unfortunately many have fallen into a pattern of not seeking God's guidance when confronted with major decisions. When it comes to discovering one's vocation, human nature can take over and we can become consumed with chasing the wrong things: money, fame, and power. Essentially, some opt to live outside of God's will—and perform tasks He has not called them to—in exchange for financial perks, comfort, and security.

The consequences of rejecting God's plan for our lives are monumental. Luke 18:18-30, for example, tells the story of a rich young ruler who retained his money but lost much more: "A certain ruler asked him, 'Good teacher, what must I do to inherit eternal life?'.... [Jesus replied], 'Sell everything you have and give to the poor, and you will have treasure in heaven. Then come, follow me.' When he heard this, he became very sad, because he was a man of great wealth."

When attempting to discern our vocational calling, it is important to face up to reality. Instead of blindly pursuing vocational paths that do not match our gifts, we need to invite God—and those we trust—to help us identify our strengths and weaknesses. At times we can be like the kid who is batting

.100 in Little League year after year but has his sights set on being a major league baseball player. We have to be realistic about our abilities and limitations and accept the fact that there are no upper- or lower-rung jobs when it comes to fulfilling God's plan. There is only obedience.

In prayer, we must ask God to open the right vocational door. Every door that opens is not from Him. But when we are in right relationship with God, He brings our gifts, desires, calling, preparation, and an open door together at the right time.

Finding God's will is often as simple as following where peace leads us. We seek God's will through reading His Word, praying, and seeking the counsel of mature believers. But ultimately God points us in a direction with His peace. (See Matthew 7:7-8.)

Criticism

Pursuing God's will for our lives may not be well received by others because they ascribe value to vocations based on their earning power and perceived status. Moses, Noah, Nehemiah, Paul, and Mary all experienced criticism because of their obedience. But they endured because they knew God was guiding their steps.

As their stories show, opposition is not necessarily a sign that we are outside of God's will. Joseph spent time in a pit. Stephen was stoned. Paul was imprisoned. Adversity is often part of God's plan to develop character in us in preparation for what lies ahead. When we remain faithful during seasons of difficulty, God may choose to entrust us with additional responsibility. Great ministries have been born out of tragedy, setbacks, and disappointment.

A study of recent college graduates indicated that 60 percent were unfulfilled by their current employment and were looking for another job or career.[1] If we fulfill the purpose for which God created us—regardless of the cost—finding fulfillment in our employment will no longer be a challenge.

Fortunately we are not alone in this vocational journey. Just as God was with the Israelites when they traversed the desert, be assured He is with us today. Deuteronomy 2:7 says, "The Lord your God has blessed you in all the work of your hands. He has watched over your journey through this vast desert. These forty years the Lord your God has been with you, and you have not lacked anything."

ASK YOURSELF

Am I maximizing my gifts at work? If not, is God preparing me for another vocation?

ACTION PLANS

1. Invite your friends and family members to identify your vocational gifts.

2. Ask God to align your gifts with the right vocation and employment opportunity.

APPLICATION PRAYER

Dear God: Today I am raising my hand as a volunteer. If You see a task—large or small—that needs to be performed that aligns with my gifts, I am willing to try. I surrender my vocational future to You. Guide my steps. Amen.

"Ask not what your country can do for you; ask what you can do for your country."

—John F. Kennedy

CHAPTER 5

GETTING PAID WHAT YOU DESERVE

A N ESTIMATED 25 PERCENT of the workforce in the United States claims to show up to work each day simply "to collect a paycheck."[1] Because they are motivated by compensation, we can assume many of those surveyed would change jobs in a heartbeat to get a higher wage. In addition, they may feel they are not getting paid what they deserve.

Some years ago, a longtime employee at Truline Industries left the company to accept a position that offered a higher wage. In less than one month he returned, asking to be rehired for his old job. He apologetically explained that he had discovered there is more to consider than wages when selecting a job.

When evaluating a job opportunity, some ask, "What's in it for me?" For followers of Jesus, we ask two different questions: "What's in it for God?" and "What's in it for the company?" We understand that working where God wants us—and contributing to the success of the company—is more important than how much we are paid.

Second Chronicles 15:7 says, "Be strong and do not give up, for your work will be rewarded." When we give our best effort and work as unto the Lord, He promises to meet our needs. This concept is foreign to our culture, but consistent with living according to God's Word. We champion a definition of success that is different from that of non-Christians. Our measuring stick is based solely on our obedience to God.

King Solomon's definition of success was transformed in his latter years. He discovered that success did not depend on what he achieved, what he possessed, or whom he pleased; it rested solely on His relationship with God. In Ecclesiastes 2:9-11, Solomon writes, "I became greater by far than anyone in Jerusalem before me. In all this my wisdom stayed with me. I denied myself nothing my eyes desired; I refused my heart no pleasure. My heart took delight in all my work, and this was the reward for all my labor. Yet when I surveyed all that my hands had done and what I had toiled to achieve, everything was meaningless, a chasing after the wind; nothing was gained under the sun."

Solomon discovered the truth found in Psalm 127:1-2: "Unless the Lord builds the house, its builders labor in vain. Unless the Lord watches over the city, the watchmen stand guard in vain. In vain you rise early and stay up late, toiling for food to eat—for he grants sleep to those he loves."

Self-worth and Compensation

In our society, many determine their self-worth based on vocational achievement and level of compensation. Conversely, as Christians, we know our worth was declared when God sent His Son to die on a cross for our sins. God's love for us is not measured by dollar signs.

I remember reading about more than 5,000 college students who were asked to quantify their starting salary expectations following graduation. More than 80 percent anticipated a salary for their first job of over $50,000. Certainly many of those surveyed based their salary expectations on what others earn. That formula, however, only leads to ingratitude and more dissatisfaction. Fortunately God does not need a ranking system or pay scale to determine what we need or deserve. He is a sovereign God who rewards as He deems appropriate.

I have a friend who is one of the hardest workers I have seen, although he does not earn a high wage. He is faithful to the tasks he is given and generous toward others. And even though he has very few material possessions, he is content to mount up treasures in heaven. He is a testament to the fact that hard work, dedication, and determination do not guarantee monetary gain. We must remind ourselves that God is sovereign and He alone promotes and rewards.

Seeking a higher paying job is not inappropriate, but we need to ask ourselves why we are not content with what God has already provided. The Apostle Paul, in Acts 20:33-35, puts this issue in perspective: "I have not coveted anyone's silver or gold or clothing. You yourselves know that these hands of mine have supplied my own needs and the needs of my companions. In everything I did, I showed you that by this kind of hard work we must help the weak, remembering the words the Lord Jesus himself said: 'It is more blessed to give than to receive.'" Paul is saying that material rewards are not intended to merely improve our standard of living. Rather, we are commanded to use some of the resources entrusted to us to help people in need and accomplish God's work.

Seeking a higher-paying job under the guise of being able to give more money away may be faulty reasoning as well. How many times have we said, "If God blesses me I'll give generously to my church or favorite charity"? But we need to learn to give graciously in our current circumstances.

Employer's Duty

Although as employees we are to trust God for our wages and rewards, it is also incumbent on employers to fairly compensate their workers. At Truline Industries, for example, we understand our God-given responsibility to care for our employees. We take Jeremiah 22:13 seriously: "Woe to him who builds his palace by unrighteousness, his upper rooms by injustice, making his countrymen work for nothing, not paying them for their labor."

Whether God has placed you as an employer or employee, Deuteronomy 15:10 promises to reward a generous heart: "Give generously to him and do so without a grudging heart; then because of this the Lord your God will bless you in all your work and in everything you put your hand to."

Because we work for God and our wages come from Him, we can rest in the knowledge that He will take care of our needs and we will be fairly compensated for our labor.

ASK YOURSELF

Are there ways I'm spending my wages that are outside of God's will?

ACTION PLANS

1. Pull out your tax returns for the last three years and thank God for all He has provided. Tell him you are content with what you are currently earning, and ask Him where you can make some life-changes to give more now.

2. Prepare a monthly budget and evaluate whether you are sharing enough with others in need.

APPLICATION PRAYER

Dear God: Thank You for all You have provided. Help me to be satisfied with what I have. As You bless me, I pledge to give generously to Your work and to people in need. I know the depth of Your love is not measured by financial reward. If I do my part, I know You will do Yours. I rest in the confidence that You will meet all my needs. Amen.

*"Coming together is a beginning.
Keeping together is progress. Working
together is success."*

—*Henry Ford*

CHAPTER 6

WORKING IN THE
RIGHT PLACE

URING MY SENIOR YEAR at Bible college, my
family was devastated by tragedy. My younger
brother, Dean, was killed by a drunken driver. Little
did I know that the accident would change the course
of my life—and my vocation. We were still dealing
with the pain of his passing when my father asked
me to consider rejoining Truline Industries, to help
run the company. At first I resisted. My brother was
the son destined to work at the company—not me. I
had just spent four years in Bible college preparing
for a preaching ministry. But as I asked God where
He wanted me to work, it became clear that Truline
was the pulpit to which He was calling me.

For some people, job security is everything. They
want to work where they can plant their feet for 20
years. To a degree that is understandable. After all,
studies indicate that the loss of a job is the eighth
most stressful life experience.[1] But, as His children,

God provides all the job security we need. Our hearts should be so aligned with His will that we want to work where our gifts and talents can be used to their greatest potential to the glory of God. We want to be wherever He can maximize those gifts.

The job God calls us to may require, for example, accepting a 50 percent pay cut to work in a more stressful environment at a nonprofit charitable organization. He may call us to serve as an executive at a large company, where our decisions have an impact on the future of thousands of employees. Some may be promoted to positions where the financial rewards are significant and they have the opportunity to make large contributions to God's work. But whether we are serving as a nurse in a cancer ward or a missionary rescuing orphans from garbage heaps in Africa, the important issue is that we know we are in God's will.

Discernment

So how can we discern God's will concerning our place of employment?

First, like Isaiah, we need to acknowledge that God will meet our needs: "The Lord will guide you always; he will satisfy your needs in a sun-scorched land and will strengthen your frame. You will be like a well-watered garden, like a spring whose waters never fail" (Isaiah 58:11).

Second, like Jeremiah, we need to submit our will and our future to God's purposes: "I know, O Lord, that a man's life is not his own; it is not for man to direct his steps" (Jeremiah 10:23).

Third, we need to ask God to show us the next step. For our own good, He seldom reveals the entirety of His plan. At times we may feel alone, as if we are wandering aimlessly with no destination in sight. Joseph certainly wondered what he had done to be sold into slavery and be falsely accused, yet little did he know that it was all part of God's plan to promote him to a place of influence. Regardless of our proximity, circumstances or trepidation, we can rest assured we are never lost. We have access to God's GPS system and He will show us the next turn in the road. Though at times it may appear we are veering off course, we can take comfort in knowing He will never take us down the wrong road.

Fourth, we need to ask God to show us His timing. People can hear God's voice and know His will concerning where they are to work, but then assume He is calling for an immediate job change. If we don't know His will *and* His timing, the prudent course of action is to exercise patience and be still. The Apostle Paul, for example, ministered and traveled where the Holy Spirit led Him. At times he longed to go to a particular church or city, but the Holy Spirit delayed him. Paul did not fully understand the delays, but he knew the wisdom of following God's timetable.

Fifth, we need to ask God for the courage to obey Him regardless of the job location, salary, title, or function. Sometimes He takes us down short, winding roads, filled with blind turns. He may send us to a particular job to minister to one person who is facing a divorce or battling alcoholism and then, shortly thereafter, relocate us to another place of employment. That doesn't help build one's 401k, but it helps restore the lives we touch. At times, because we don't understand His purposes, it may appear that we have taken a vocational detour. We ask, "God, why did you bring me here?" But we can take comfort in knowing He has a purpose in each destination. Like David, we can pray, "Show me your ways, O Lord, teach me your paths; guide me in your truth and teach me, for you are God my Savior, and my hope is in you all day long" (Psalm 25:4-5).

Many employees torture themselves over the question, "Where should I work?" Instead, Jesus says, in Matthew 6:33-34, to submit our future—including our place of employment—to His care: "But seek first his kingdom and his righteousness, and all these things will be given to you as well. Therefore do not worry about tomorrow, for tomorrow will worry about itself. Each day has enough trouble of its own."

ASK YOURSELF

What things can I do to improve my work environment?

ACTION PLANS

1. Write a list of coworkers who need encouragement, salvation, and God's guidance.

2. Write a list of worries related to your job. Then, as a sign that you are entrusting these concerns to God, throw the list away.

APPLICATION PRAYER

Dear God: I confess that I've been too worried about where I should work. Help me to surrender this matter to You. And help me understand that where I work is not as important as the fact I am working for You. Give me the courage to be an instrument of Your grace to coworkers that You have sent my way. Amen.

"Whatever your life's work is, do it well. A man should do his job so well that the living, the dead, and the unborn could do it no better."

—Martin Luther King, Jr.

CHAPTER 7

IMPROVING YOUR PRODUCTION AT WORK

THOUSANDS OF EMPLOYEES PARTICIPATED in a poll to determine the hardest workers in America. Small business owners received the most votes; government workers received the least.[1] I was never employed by the government, but for most of my life I would have fallen into the "least working" category. When I committed my life to Jesus, however, and began to read about His life, I felt convicted of my poor work ethic. Jesus gave 100 percent. He gave His life. He invested in the lives of people. He did everything well. Meanwhile, I was coasting through my workdays at 50 percent of my capacity. I came to the realization that I owed it to God—and my employer—to give my all.

If I wanted to fulfill God's destiny for my life, I had to commit my work hours to God, too. I needed to become as passionate about my job as I was about watching the Cleveland Browns or skiing in Aspen,

Colorado, with my family. Proverbs 14:23 says, "All hard work brings a profit, but mere talk leads only to poverty."

For many Americans, hard work has become something to avoid. The "good life" is portrayed in movies as lounging around a swimming pool with your feet up, sipping lemonade, and fielding an occasional work-related telephone call. Infomercials tout "get rich" methods that promise a high return with little effort. But these images are contrary to the Word of God. Proverbs 18:9 says, "One who is slack in his work is brother to one who destroys."

God and Hard Work

Contrary to popular opinion, God is not opposed to hard work. He did not necessarily deliver the Israelites from the rock quarries in Egypt, for example, simply because Pharaoh was working them too hard; they were delivered because they were not being permitted to freely worship God.

Employees owe their employer *and* their Creator a hard day's work. Yet, the average employee works 45 hours a week, of which approximately 17 hours are unproductive.[2] That is like the basketball player who shows little effort and production for three quarters but then somehow propels himself to score 20 points in the fourth quarter. You can't help asking, "Where's he been?" Sometimes God has every right to ask us the same question.

What would happen if a professional athlete—or any employee for that matter—walked into the business owner's office and offered to return a portion of his or her salary for not giving maximum effort? Most likely, the owner would gladly accept the refund and the other employees would complain, because they expect to be compensated whether they give 100 percent or not.

Even though our employer may not require us to punch a clock—and the company is satisfied with our performance—we should work as if God is looking over our shoulder. He knows whether we have earned the right to cash our paycheck, based on our effort and production. Nothing is more important than satisfying Him and meeting His expectations. His blessing depends on it. When we give 100 percent we honor God and show proper respect to our employer. When we surrender to lazy tendencies and give less effort, we jeopardize God's favor on our finances.

Severe Consequences

Proverbs 21:25-26 describes the consequences of violating God's principles related to work: "The sluggard's craving will be the death of him, because his hands refuse to work. All day long he craves for more, but the righteous give without sparing."

Obviously it is impossible to give 110 percent, but I have met a few workers who try to set Guinness records in the workplace. In the end, they lose balance and make their employer happy at the expense of their family and church life. God only requires that we give 100 percent. If our employer demands more than we can give—and we are honest with ourselves and with God—we have an obligation to inform our supervisor that we have reached our maximum capacity. In response, the supervisor may instruct us to clean out our desk, but that is beyond our control. If that occurs, at least we can leave with our head held high, knowing we have honored God with our work ethic and performance.

It pleases God when believers have a reputation among their fellow employees for excellence and hard work. It is not a coincidence that those workers who are motivated by service to God and a desire to be a godly example to others also tend to earn promotions. God takes care of those who serve Him by giving 100 percent on the job.

ASK YOURSELF

Which work habits are limiting my production on the job?

ACTION PLANS

1. Invite your supervisor to identify areas of your work that need improvement.

2. Develop a plan for improving areas of weakness on the job, such as seeking more education and training.

APPLICATION PRAYER

Dear God: I confess that there are times I have not given maximum effort at work. Thank You for Your forgiveness. I want to glorify You through my work ethic and excellence on the job. Show me areas that need improvement and give me the willpower to shore up those weaknesses. And help me keep my life in balance between work, family, and church. Amen.

"If I had eight hours to chop down a tree, I'd spend six sharpening my ax."

—*Abraham Lincoln*

Chapter 8

Winning Over Your Coworkers

A LEADING EXPERT IN HUMAN resources was asked to identify the top eight causes of conflict in the workplace. He cited conflicting needs, styles, perceptions, goals, pressures, roles, values, and policies.[1]

Escaping all conflict is unlikely, but Christians should endeavor to keep it to a minimum. We may not agree with everyone, but we should remain civil, humble, honorable, and respectful in our disagreements. We should seek to understand before seeking to be understood. First Thessalonians 4:11-12 says, "Make it your ambition to lead a quiet life, to mind your own business and to work with your hands, just as we told you, so that your daily life may win the respect of outsiders and so that you will not be dependent on anybody." Romans 12:18 says, "If it is possible, as far as it depends on you, live at peace with everyone."

As Christians in the workplace we are targets. Unwittingly some coworkers may be used by our spiritual enemy to attack our credibility and reputation. Nevertheless, we must respond with grace, because they do not have a relationship with Christ. They are working with different goals and priorities. Jesus commanded us to love our enemies and pray for those who persecute us (Matthew 5:44). That means we should work toward—and hope for—their success, too.

Matthew 5:16 says, "Let your light shine before men, that they may see your good deeds and praise your Father in heaven." To live out that scripture, our names should be associated among our coworkers with qualities like humility, hard work, honesty, and helpfulness. That doesn't just happen. It is a by-product of our relationship with Christ.

They Are Watching

Coworkers watch how we live and work. They hear what we say and see how we treat others, especially in times of crisis and conflict. They have observed so much legalism and hypocrisy through the years that often cynicism prevents them from giving us the benefit of the doubt. In some cases, they will assume the worst. Because we are representatives of Jesus, we need to be persons they admire and want to emulate. It goes without saying, we cannot claim to be a follower of Christ and cheat our employer or mistreat the employees under our supervision. We cannot violate a biblical code without reinforcing coworkers' skepticism of Christians.

God wants us to be people of influence in the workplace. That does not necessarily mean He wants us to be president of the company. He's more concerned that we have a positive impact on the lives of coworkers than that we have a corner office with a spectacular view of the city. Influence is not defined by position; it is defined by integrity. Some Christians, due to pride and fear, keep their distance from nonbelievers. That is contrary to the way Jesus lived. He spent His life engaging nonbelievers in conversation. He led with grace, mercy, and friendship, rather than with condemnation. He didn't make them feel inferior because of their sin and shortcomings. Without compromising who He was, He focused on building relationships with people whom the Father brought along His path.

Judgment and Grace

We had one employee who certainly saw the work-place as a mission field, but his methods for evangelism bordered on condemnation. He preached punishment rather than grace. Furthermore, at times he portrayed himself as sinless and made others feel guilty for their failures. Even Christians did their best to avoid him. Sadly, he scrutinized the behavior of one new believer to the point where the employee walked away from his faith altogether. Eventually both men left our company.

On the other hand, God brought us another employee who understood how to represent Christ in the workplace. He had immigrated to this country and had earned his master's degree, but he was having difficulty finding employment as a teacher. I felt God nudging me to hire him at Truline Industries to work in the factory until he could find a teaching posi-tion. Though we assumed his tenure with us would be short, we trained him to run some of the equip-ment. After several weeks on the job, he made an appointment to meet with me. He said, "I've decided I don't want to return to teaching. If there's a job for me here, then I'm convinced this is where God wants me to be." When I asked him what had led him to this decision, he said, "There are people on the factory floor who need Jesus. I can share with them God's love. I am needed here." I thought, *Here's a man who understands that God is his employer.* We agreed to hire him, and he became an unofficial chaplain—a person employees know they can go to when they need advice and prayer.

Here are some steps we can take to build relationships with our coworkers and represent Jesus on the job:

1. Pray for a different coworker each day.

2. Compliment someone's work each day.

3. Celebrate others' successes. Rejoice with them.

4. When conflict arises, do not gossip about it to other people. Talk to the individual with whom you have disagreement.

5. Don't let differences fester or employ the "silent treatment." Buy the other person a cup of coffee and talk it out.

6. Give one another the benefit of the doubt.

7. If a person cannot be trusted, pray God changes his or her heart.

8. Give others reason to trust you.

9. Stay positive—don't fall into a pattern of complaining and criticizing.

10. Give second chances.

ASK YOURSELF

Are there any coworkers with whom I have conflict, and what can I do to heal that relationship?

ACTION PLANS

1. If you have offended someone—or he or she has offended you take the steps necessary to get the matter resolved.

2. Ask God to give you opportunities each day to represent Jesus to a nonbeliever.

APPLICATION PRAYER

Dear God: Guard my back from those who want to disparage my name. Give me the wisdom to know when to speak and when to remain silent. Help me to befriend those who don't share my faith. And help me to pray each day for my coworkers, that they would discover Your love and accept Your gift of salvation. Amen.

"The only advice my Dad's given me is:
If you ain't having fun, it ain't working,
so always have fun with what you're
doing. If you don't love it then there's
no reason to do it. And don't do it
for fame or money—do it because it's
something that you feel is right."

—*Miley Cyrus*

CHAPTER 9

PREPARING YOUR CHILDREN TO WORK

A PHYSICIAN HAD HIGH HOPES for his four-year-old daughter. One day his child picked up his stethoscope and began playing with it. The proud father immediately exclaimed, "Look, my daughter wants to follow in my footsteps." Then the child lifted the instrument to her mouth and said: "Welcome to McDonald's. May I take your order?"[1]

As parents, we all want the best for our children. But, more often than not, that does not happen without parental training and godly examples. Teaching is not just what we say; it's what we live. Proverbs 22:6 says, "Train a child in the way he should go, and when he is old he will not turn from it."

Values Worth Teaching

Following are eight values related to work that every parent should instill in their children:

1. Teach children that work was created by God for our benefit. Work is not an obligation; it is a privilege. God is our ultimate Employer and Provider.

As parents, we must not arrive home and complain day after day to our children about our job, coworkers, or supervisor. That sends the wrong message. Often it conditions them to be miserable with their work someday and shows them an improper way to deal with adversity. Instead, children need to see their parents committing their work-related challenges to the Lord in prayer.

2. Teach children to respect authority. Although they do not have an employer, teach them to exhibit respect for their teachers at school and their pastors at church. Teach them how to show respect and appreciation for waiters, service providers, neighbors, their peers, themselves, and others.

3. Teach children that God has given them a unique set of gifts and talents. The adage that "they can be anything *they* want to be" is untrue. The goal is to be what God wants them to be. Unfortunately they are being conditioned through television and other mediums to aspire to be rock musicians, professional athletes, Hollywood actors, and other kinds of "stars." Although there is nothing inherently wrong with those professions, as parents, we need to help our children discover a wide range of vocations. We can help them discern their callings by identifying their gifts. This will require a commitment to reading God's Word together, to reinforce that God has a destiny for their lives that may be different from what is portrayed on television.

4. Teach children that their value to God and their parents is not based on what vocation they choose or how much money they earn. Regardless of how successful they are in the classroom or in athletics, they are loved unconditionally. They will make mistakes. They will make wrong turns. But they will never escape God's grace or their parents' love.

5. Teach children to give God their best. Explain to them that if they received a gift of $1 million, they wouldn't take the money and bury it in the back yard. Some might invest it; others might spend every dollar. Likewise God has given them gifts and talents to be spent for His glory. Help them understand that when you say you want them to "reach their potential," you are actually saying you want them to see "God's gifts maximized in their life."

6. Teach children responsibility. My sons have two types of responsibilities: paid and unpaid. Because we operate a farm and we want to teach our boys the principles of earning and managing money, they are paid for feeding the animals and cutting the hay. Through this arrangement they have learned that because God has blessed me with a job, I can in turn compensate them. They aren't working as a favor to Mom and Dad; they're working for God. And He provides their wages. Conversely, their unpaid duties include setting the dinner table, cleaning their room, and taking out the trash. In return for these chores, they get to eat three meals a day and sleep in a warm bed.

For this system to be effective, though, parents must hold their children accountable for work quality and timeliness. When standards aren't met, discipline is necessary. Parents must be careful when administering discipline and avoid going to extremes. Obviously we do not want to harm a child's self-esteem. Ephesians 6:4 says, "Fathers, do not exasperate your children; instead, bring them up in the training and instruction of the Lord."

7. Teach children the value of a dollar. Show them the impact they can have on the lives of others through generosity and wise stewardship. Let them see firsthand through mission trips how others survive without adequate food and shelter.

8. Teach children to give to God. Our children have been taught to give 10 percent of their wages and gifts to God's work and to designate 10 percent for savings. The remaining 80 percent is theirs to spend as they choose, although they understand that God has an interest in that, too. Through our example, we have also tried to teach them to give God their time by volunteering at church or in other places in the community. We want them to know the meaning of Matthew 6:19-21: "Do not store up for yourselves treasures on earth, where moth and rust destroy, and where thieves break in and steal. But store up for yourselves treasures in heaven, where moth and rust do not destroy, and where thieves do not break in and steal. For where your treasure is, there your heart will be also."

Children are God's gift to parents. They have been entrusted to us to mold them in the ways of the Lord. They require work, patience, and persistence. But few things in life bring as much joy and satisfaction as seeing your children working unto God.

ASK YOURSELF

What are my vocational expectations for my child, and are they realistic?

ACTION PLANS

1. Let your child work alongside you on a project such as pulling weeds in the yard or washing the family car. This will give you an opportunity to discuss the biblical principles of work.

2. Write out a list of unpaid chores for your child and deadlines for their completion. Then prepare a list of jobs for which they will be compensated. Use this as an opportunity to teach a life lesson.

APPLICATION PRAYER

Dear God: Thank You for the gift of children. Give me wisdom as I raise them to follow You. Help me teach them the principles of work and generosity. Protect them from the influences that would threaten their relationship with You and hinder their future work. Make our home a place where they can experience grace and discipline. Amen.

"By working faithfully eight hours a day, you may eventually get to be a boss and work twelve hours a day."

—*Robert Frost*

CHAPTER 10

"RETIRING" AT THE RIGHT TIME

How often have we heard someone say, "I never have enough time" or "I have too much work to do"? Unfortunately, if they're like the average American, they're also spending four hours each night watching television. That's 28 hours a week and equates to 9 years of a person's life.[1] Typically our workload is not the problem. Our greater challenge is time management and our tendency to coast toward retirement.

Leisure time—rather than work—has become the priority for many Americans. If they are paid for 40 hours of labor, they are reluctant to put in more time without further compensation. It's more important to rush home to play a video game or get in an extra hole of golf than it is to complete a task for their employer.

Conversely, some people work so many hours that their family life and church attendance suffer. They forget the commandment found in Exodus 20:8-10: "Remember the Sabbath day by keeping it holy. Six days you shall labor and do all your work, but the seventh day is a Sabbath to the Lord your God. On it you shall not do any work."

I have heard that nearly 60 percent of Americans do not attend church on a typical weekend. One of the primary reasons stated for not attending church is one's "workload" or "the need to rest because of excessive work."

Spending the Sabbath

Man was not made for the Sabbath; the Sabbath was made for man. God knew we needed a day of "retirement" to recharge our batteries—physically, spiritually, and emotionally. He commands us to set aside one day each week for rest and reflection—to spend it in ways that honor Him and help us gain perspective. Too often our "leisure time" is spent running so fast or abusing our credit cards that it only serves to increase our level of stress.

Each day we need to find a way to be still for at least 15 minutes to simply listen to God's voice. Jesus took time to commune with the Father. He found a place of quietude to receive instruction and perspective.

Many today have taken a much different approach: they retreat to the couch and escape by watching sitcoms. But it is difficult to hear God speaking to our hearts if He's limited to the commercial breaks.

There are 168 hours in a week. One fourth of our week is dedicated to work. But how we spend the remaining 128 hours has a bearing on how productive we are for God and our employer. We need to ask ourselves if we are managing our time wisely and doing the things that foster stamina and balance:

1. Are we getting adequate sleep?

2. Are we attending church?

3. Are we exercising?

4. Are we spending quality time with our family?

5. Are we praying and reading God's Word?

6. Are we investing in relationships that allow us to edify others and share our faith?

Life's Ultimate Goal?

Some workers see formal retirement as the finish line—life's ultimate goal. They contribute to a 401k and have already selected their retirement community. There is nothing unspiritual about that, but it's important to note that there are no biblical examples of people who entered retirement and ceased to be productive. To the contrary, until they passed into eternity, Moses led his people, David served as king, and the Apostle Paul continued preaching.

Most workers over age 67 plan to continue working to "remain mentally engaged." The problem is that society doesn't always give appropriate honor to senior citizens and tends to limit their vocational opportunities—even though according to U.S. statistics, life expectancy has grown from 60 in 1935 to 76 in 2008. Many seniors feel they have been "put on the shelf" against their will. They would prefer to remain active in volunteer service, but they also don't want people to feel obligated to give them a position. They simply want to fill a needed role.

Retirement is not as much an event on the calendar as it is a progression of life from a primary vocation to a secondary one. It should be viewed as a time God has given "retirees" to invest in nurturing relationships. Their focus must remain on bearing fruit and passing on knowledge and experience to younger generations. Titus 2:6-7 says, "Encourage the young men to be self-controlled. In everything set them an example by doing what is good."

There are a myriad of volunteer opportunities for senior citizens in local churches and with nonprofit service organizations. And there is a pressing need for focused prayer and letter writing that encourages young people, pastors, and frontline missionaries. Regardless of what we choose to do for the Lord, the goal is not retirement. The objective is continued productivity.

If you or someone you know wants an opportunity to remain productive, here are some steps that can be taken:

1. Notify your pastor of your willingness to volunteer your time to the church (e.g., teaching a class, working in the office, visiting guests, etc.)

2. Make a list of local charities. Notify them of your willingness to serve. (Prepare a resume with skills and references.)

3. Locate a political candidate you believe in whom you can assist by making phone calls or working in the office.

4. Offer to serve as a tutor at a local school.

5. Volunteer to mentor young people through local social agencies.

6. Commit to joining with others to pray for churches, ministries, charities, etc.

A Father's Blessing

Retirement was a major adjustment for my father. He had grown accustomed to working 70- to 80-hour weeks and making sure the factory was operating at full capacity. When he committed his life to Jesus, he cut back on his schedule and closed the factory on Sundays. Today he seldom comes to the office, devoting more of his time to traveling and building relationships. But his continued influence on my life is critical to the success of Truline Industries. His prayers, insights, and words of encouragement help sustain me. From my perspective, he didn't retire; he simply transitioned to a different set of responsibilities.

I work about half as many hours as my father did, and my management style is dissimilar, too. Yet, my father is my biggest cheerleader. His words of affirmation and support mean a great deal. But nothing compares to knowing that God is pleased by my worship at work. Hopefully one day, when I enter the Pearly Gates and report for duty, I'll stand before my Lord and Savior and hear Him say, "Job well done."

ASK YOURSELF

Am I giving 100 percent on the job? And what plans do I have to remain productive after retirement?

ACTION PLANS

1. Monitor how you use your leisure time for one week, and ask yourself if you are using it wisely.

2. Find a retiree and give him or her an opportunity to serve.

APPLICATION PRAYER

Dear God: Time is precious and I want my leisure time to be beneficial. Help me manage my time and take advantage of moments that I can be still before You. Direct me to senior citizens who are willing to spiritually invest in my life. And help me not to view retirement as an extended period of leisure. Instead help me to remain productive all the days of my life. Amen.

ENDNOTES

Introduction

1. Anonymous, "U.S. Job Satisfaction Keeps Falling," Business Credit (April 1, 2005).

Chapter 1
Getting Motivated to Work

1. *Merriam-Webster's Collegiate Dictionary,* 11th Edition, "work," 1b.

Chapter 2
Working for the Right Boss

1. http://www.quotemonk.com/quotes/work_quotes. htm (accessed October 4, 2008).

2. Michelle Nichols, "Many Workers Do Not Respect Their Bosses," http://www.reuters.com/article/ / idUSTRE4957B020081006 (accessed on October 27, 2010).

3. Nancy Leigh DeMoss, *Brokenness: The Heart God Revives.* Chicago: Moody Publishers (2002, 2005).

Chapter 3
Coping With a Miserable Job

1. Gregory P. Smith, "Top-Ten Reasons Why People Quit Their Jobs," http://www.businessknowhow.com/ manage/whyquit.htm (accessed October 4, 2008).

Chapter 4
Finding the Perfect Job

1. Heather Huhman, "Survey: Most recent graduates leave first jobs within two years," http://www.examiner.com/x-828-Entry-Level-Careers-Examiner~y2008m9d5-Survey-Most-recent-graduates-leave-first-jobs-within-two-years (accessed September 5, October 5, 2008).

Chapter 5
Getting Paid What You Deserve

1. Business Wire, "CollegeHire Survey Finds Salary Expectations At All-time High for Class of 2001; Top Dollar is Top Priority According to More Than 5,000 Computer Science and Computer Engineering Students," http://findarticles.com/p/articles/mi_m0EIN/is_2000_August_14/ai_64146060/print?tag=artBody;col1 (accessed August 14, 2000 & October 5, 2008).

Chapter 6
Working in the Right Place

1. Bruce Weinstein, BusinessWeek, quoted by Jesse Nunes in "The Ethics of Downsizing," http://www.boston.com/jobs/blog/ (accessed October 1 &, 4, 2008).

Chapter 7
Improving Your Production at Work

1. Rasmussen Reports, "Adults Say Small Business Owners are the Hardest Workers," http://www.rasmussenreports.com/public_content/business/general_business/adults_say_small_business_owners_are_the_hardest_workers (accessed on September 4 & October 4, 2008).

2. "Survey Finds Workers Average Only Three Productive Days per Week," http://www.microsoft.com/presspass/press/2005/mar05/03-15threeproductivedayspr.mspx. (accessed on March 15, 2005 & October 4, 2008).

Chapter 8
Winning Over Your Co-Workers

1. Julie Gatlin, Allen Wysocki, and Karl Kepner, "Understanding Conflict in the Workplace," http://edis.ifas.ufl.edu/HR024 (accessed October 5, 2008).

Chapter 9
Preparing Your Children to Work

1. http://www.butlerwebs.com/jokes/kids.htm (accessed October 4, 2008).

Chapter 10
"Retiring" at the Right Time

1. A.C. Nielsen Co., quoted in "Television and Health," http://www.csun.edu/science/health/docs/tv&health.html (accessed on October 4, 2008).

About the Author

Court Durkalski is CEO of Truline Industries, a multimillion-dollar jet parts manufacturing company located in Chesterland, Ohio. A graduate of Valley Forge Christian College, Court is a highly regarded speaker and business strategist. His company has been built on Christian business principles, including placing a high value on each customer, supplier, and employee. He acknowledges that Truline Industries and its resources belong to God, and challenges other business leaders and workers to see their work as a form of worship.

Court serves as president of a Teen Challenge board and a director on the Convoy of Hope board of directors. He, his wife Amy, and their two sons are also active in their local church.

IF YOU'RE A FAN OF THIS BOOK, PLEASE TELL OTHERS…

- Write about *Winning at Work* on your blog, Twitter, MySpace, and Facebook page.

- Suggest *Winning at Work* to friends.

- When you're in a bookstore, ask them if they carry the book. The book is available through all major distributors, so any bookstore that does not have *Winning at Work* in stock can easily order it.

- Write a positive review of *Winning at Work* on www.amazon.com.

- Send my publisher, HigherLife Publishing, suggestions on Web sites, conferences, and events you know of where this book could be offered at media@ahigherlife.com.

- Purchase additional copies to give away as gifts.

CONNECT WITH ME...

To contact Court Durkalski or to schedule him for a speaking engagement, please visit **winning-at-work.org.**

You may also contact my publisher directly:

HigherLife Publishing
400 Fontana Circle
Building 1 – Suite 105
Oviedo, Florida 32765
Phone: (407) 563-4806
Email: media@ahigherlife.com